FUNNY HOW my LIFE WORKS
JOURNAL

GUIDED BY
MICHAEL JR.

"Exceptionally gifted at combining story with thought-provoking life principles, Michael Jr. exhibits what it means to be a comedic thought leader. Using comedy and dynamic storytelling, he brings laughter and encouragement to audiences all over the world as he inspires audiences to discover and activate their purpose. This unique skill set has landed him on stages like The Tonight Show on NBC, Tedx Talks, and Jimmy Kimmel Live. You can find him in Sony Pictures' feature film *War Room*, as well as starring roles in *Selfie Dad, Laughing On Purpose* and *More Than Funny*."

PRAISE FOR FUNNY HOW LIFE WORKS

In a time when we need hope and humor more than anything, Michael Jr. delivers both in droves.
–Andy Stanley. Author, communicator and founder of North Point Ministries

Michael Jr. is exceptionally gifted at combining funny stories and spiritual principles. He will have you laughing and crying on the same page.
–Craig Groeschel. Pastor of Life Church and *New York Times* Best-selling Author

If you want to laugh and learn and see the world differently, read this book.
–Jon Acuff. *New York Times* Best-selling Author of **Finish: Give Yourself the Gift of Done**

INTRODUCTION

We all read great books like *Funny How Life Works* and think "I should do that".

The problem is, we put the book down, walk away and forget about all the good things we could have made part of our life.

Whether you have completed the book, just started, or haven't gotten your copy yet - begin journaling today.

This journal will help you take all the good things about *Funny How Life Works* and actually APPLY them to YOUR life.

Take each chapter one by one. Relate to it personally. Make a change.

If you go through this process, you will not be the same person in the end.

The format follows the way Michael Jr. creates comedy. Improv. Premise. Punchline. Michael Jr. shares how life parallels comedy with this process. The Improv in this case is what happened in the moment. The Premise involves you addressing the issue. The Punchline is where YOU move forward as a better person.

CHAPTER 1

60 CENTS AND AN ORANGE

Despair and disappointment have a way of sapping our strength and ambushing our ambition. But allow me to suggest that maybe something deeper is happening through the struggle. Perhaps you're learning a lesson that is actually preparing you, developing you, and equipping you for something else down the road.

> *We are pressed on every side by troubles, but we are not crushed. We are perplexed, but not driven to despair.*
> *–2 Corinthians 4:8*

IMPROV

Reflect on a moment of despair in your past. What made the moment affect you so greatly?

PREMISE

Did you learn from your moment of despair? If so, what did you learn? If not, how does that moment continue to affect you?

PUNCHLINE

How will you use your experience to make your life or the lives of others better in the future?

_____
_____
_____
_____
_____
_____
_____

I AM COMMITTING TO

I will resist despair by:

_____
_____
_____
_____

Date:

CHAPTER 2

AN UNOPENED GIFT

Looking back, I now realize that many of the things I resented or found annoying about my earthly father are the very things that allowed me to open the gifts my Heavenly Father had deposited in me.

Life can only be understood backwards; but it must be lived forwards.
–Soren Kierkegaard

IMPROV

Explain a part of your childhood that you found terribly unfair at the time.

PREMISE

Looking back, how have time and maturity changed your view of events?

PUNCHLINE

What else from your past can you reframe and look at differently?

_____
_____
_____
_____
_____
_____

I AM COMMITTING TO

I will change my view of this one thing in my life:

_____
_____
_____
_____

Date:

YOUR REFLECTIONS

Look back over your entries from this week.

What thoughts or feelings are strongest for you?

_____
_____
_____
_____
_____
_____
_____
_____
_____
_____
_____
_____
_____
_____
_____
_____

YOUR REFLECTIONS

What changes are you most proud of making?

CHAPTER 3

COME OUT OF THE PIT

Whether it's in your career, a relationship, raising your children, or in regard to a talent or dream, as long as you settle for "just good enough," you're spending time in the pit when God has so much more available to you.

There is no passion to be found in settling for a life that is less than the one you are capable of living.
–Nelson Mandela

IMPROV

Who do you know that has obviously settled for less in their life? How does that affect their overall happiness?

PREMISE

What area of your life are you settling in?

PUNCHLINE

How could your life be different if you refused to settle?

_____
_____
_____
_____
_____
_____

I AM COMMITTING TO

I will immediately stop settling for less by:

_____
_____
_____
_____

Date:

CHAPTER 4

THE VOICE THAT SAVED MY LIFE WITHOUT SAYING ANYTHING

Wise decisions lead to progress and accomplishment, but bad decisions can be devastating.

It is in your moments of decision that your destiny is shaped.
–Tony Robbins

IMPROV

What bad decisions do you think still affect your life today?

PREMISE

What is the best decision you ever made and why?

PUNCHLINE

What happens to your mind and emotions when you make better decisions?

I AM COMMITTING TO

I will make better decisions by:

Date:

CHAPTER 5

FUNNY THING ABOUT HAVING A GUN TO YOUR HEAD

I believe that anger preserves and intensifies pain or past hurts. The sooner we can let it go, the faster our hearts will heal and grow.

Get rid of all bitterness, rage, anger, harsh words, and slander, as well as all types of evil behavior. Instead, be kind to each other, tenderhearted, forgiving one another, just as God through Christ has forgiven you.
Ephesians 4:31–32

IMPROV

Anger eats away at people. Talk about an angry person in your life or of your acquaintance. What good parts of life has anger robbed from them?

PREMISE

Think of a time when you let anger go. How are you different now that you are not holding onto the bitterness and rage?

PUNCHLINE

How would your life be different if you had no anger or resentment?

_____
_____
_____
_____
_____
_____
_____

I AM COMMITTING TO

I release my anger about:

_____
_____
_____
_____

Date:

CHAPTER 6

A TRIP TO THE MOVIES THAT CHANGED EVERYTHING

The question isn't, Will an opportunity present itself? The question is, What will you do when it does?

> *If a window of opportunity appears, don't pull down the shade.*
> –Tom Peters

IMPROV

What opportunity have you missed in life?

PREMISE

What opportunity in life are you glad you embraced?

PUNCHLINE

How do you recognize and embrace good opportunities?

_____
_____
_____
_____
_____
_____
_____

I AM COMMITTING TO

I will open my eyes to good opportunities by:

_____
_____
_____
_____

Date:

YOUR REFLECTIONS

Look back over your entries from this week.

What thoughts or feelings are strongest for you?

_____
_____
_____
_____
_____
_____
_____
_____
_____
_____
_____
_____
_____
_____
_____

YOUR REFLECTIONS

What changes are you most proud of making?

CHAPTER 7

I WASN'T READY TO HEADLINE

I tell you that story because...sometimes I think we are so anxious to get to a destination that we overlook the importance of the process.

Success is a journey, not a destination. The doing is often more important than the outcome.
–Arthur Ashe

IMPROV

When have you been so busy trying to accomplish something that you stopped enjoying life in the process?

PREMISE

What journey did you enjoy so much the end didn't matter?

PUNCHLINE

How much joy would you have if the journey was the goal?

I AM COMMITTING TO

I will slow down and embrace the process in this area of my life:

Date:

CHAPTER 8

MEATBALL SUBS AND MY FOUR-DOOR APARTMENT

I came to understand that my ability to make people laugh was no accident, and I am to use this gift for something much bigger than just me. I discovered that and now know that I am funny for a reason.

The two most important days in your life are the day you are born and the day you find out why.
–Mark Twain

IMPROV

Who do you know that clearly understands what their purpose is? What shows you they understand their purpose?

PREMISE

What moments of clarity about your own purpose have you experienced?

PUNCHLINE

How is your quality of life improved when you are walking in your purpose?

_____

_____

_____

_____

_____

_____

I AM COMMITTING TO

I will spend _____ minutes each day reflecting or journaling about my purpose because:

_____

_____

_____

Date:

CHAPTER 9

THE TONIGHT SHOW PICKED ME

Opportunity is sneakier than that. You have to be ready and prepared in advance so when the moment comes, you can seize your opportunity.

So be careful how you live. Don't live like fools, but like those who are wise. Make the most of every opportunity in these evil days. Don't act thoughtlessly, but undestand what the Lord wants you to do.
–Ephesians 5:15–17 NLT

IMPROV

What opportunity have you had to say "no" to because you were not ready?

PREMISE

Write about an instance in your life when you KNEW you were well prepared for the opportunity presented to you.

PUNCHLINE

How would it feel to be ready when the next opportunity comes your way?

I AM COMMITTING TO

I will prepare for future opportunity by:

Date:

CHAPTER 10

THE HYSTERICAL JOKE THAT WASN'T FUNNY

Someone out there needs to hear your story, and you need to let it out.

Other people are going to find healing in your wounds. Your greatest life messages and your most effective ministry will come out of your deepest hurts.
–Rick Warren

IMPROV

What part of your life do you to keep to yourself because it causes you pain or embarrassment?

PREMISE

Think of a time when a friend or mentor shared a vulnerable story about themselves. How did it affect you?

PUNCHLINE

How could your story help others heal or improve?

_____
_____
_____
_____
_____
_____

I AM COMMITTING TO

I will share part of my story with:

_____
_____
_____
_____

Date:

CHAPTER 11

OUT OF GAS

In the pursuit of your dreams, random, unexpected things can come along at just the right time to give you the push you need exactly when you need it.

Trust in the Lord with all your heart and lean not on your own understanding.
–Proverbs 3:5

IMPROV

Describe an event in your life where you seemed to have no way out.

PREMISE

What unexpected thing happened to get you out of your circumstance?

PUNCHLINE

When you reach the end of the road, how will you remain steady and look for the unexpected?

_____
_____
_____
_____
_____
_____
_____

I AM COMMITTING TO

Regardless of how things may seem, I will keep an open mind about:

_____
_____
_____

Date:

CHAPTER 12

THE UNEXPECTED RESPONSE TO A RACIST HECKLER

Never allow the heckler's voice to determine your choice.

Don't let the noise of others' opinions drown out your own inner voice.
–Steve Jobs

IMPROV

How often do you let the opinions of others affect your life?

THE UNEXPECTED RESPONSE TO A RACIST HECKLER

PREMISE

Write about an instance where you listened to what you knew was best rather than let someone else influence you negatively.

PUNCHLINE

How is your life better when you listen to your heart?

_____
_____
_____
_____
_____
_____

I AM COMMITTING TO

I will resist the negative influence of others by:

_____
_____
_____
_____

Date:

YOUR REFLECTIONS

Look back over your entries from this week.

What thoughts or feelings are strongest for you?

_____
_____
_____
_____
_____
_____
_____
_____
_____
_____
_____
_____
_____
_____
_____

YOUR REFLECTIONS

What changes are you most proud of making?

CHAPTER 13

MY BIG BREAK

Are you asking, "What can I give?" Or, are you asking the default question, "What can I get?" If you don't choose which of these questions to ask, you will by nature ask, "What can I get?" When you make the decision to change your question, I guarantee you will find some much better answers.

Your true worth is determined by how much more you give in value than you take in payment.
–Bob Burg

IMPROV

Think of someone who seems only concerned about what they can get. Are they content? What is your opinion of them?

PREMISE

Name three people in your life who give more than expected of them. How are they viewed by their friends and family?

PUNCHLINE

How do you feel when you give more than is expected of you?

_____
_____
_____
_____
_____
_____
_____

I AM COMMITTING TO

Today, I will give a little extra by:

_____
_____
_____
_____

Date:

CHAPTER 14

FOUR $20 BOOKS FOR $16,000

...some of the greatest things in life happen outside of our comfort zones.

If you are not willing to risk the unusual, you will have to settle for the ordinary.
–Jim Rohn

IMPROV

What comfort zone are you living in, and why do you stay there?

PREMISE

Think of a time when you took a risk and stepped out of your comfort zone.

PUNCHLINE

How would your life be different if you stepped out of your current comfort zone?

_____
_____
_____
_____
_____
_____

I AM COMMITTING TO

Ask a trusted friend what comfort zone they think is holding you back.

_____
_____
_____

Date:

CHAPTER 15

BUT CAN YOU BE FUNNY IN PRISON?

Life is like a bow and arrow: the tighter the tension in the bow (the farther you've been set back), the farther the arrow will land (the farther you're going to reach). When you let go of what's behind you, you are free to soar forward.

So when life is dragging you back with difficulties, it means that it's going to launch you into something great. So just focus, and keep aiming.
–Paulo Coelho

IMPROV

What situation in your life has felt like a disadvantage when you compare your life to others?

PREMISE

Turn the situation around and explore what that seeming disadvantage has prompted you to do.

PUNCHLINE

How is the disadvantage actually a blessing? Has it pushed you to overcome? Has it allowed you to help others with the same disadvantage?

_____
_____
_____
_____
_____
_____
_____

I AM COMMITTING TO

I will benefit from my disadvantage this week by:

_____
_____
_____
_____

Date:

CHAPTER 16

I MADE A SUPERHERO LAUGH

I have the gift of helping people laugh, but a gift isn't really a gift until you give it away expecting nothing in return.

> *You have not lived today until you have done something for someone who can never repay you.*
> *–John Bunyan*

IMPROV

Think of someone who has helped you while expecting absolutely nothing in return. How did they make you feel?

PREMISE

Did being helped by someone else inspire you to help others?

PUNCHLINE

What is the benefit to YOU of helping someone who can never repay you?

_____
_____
_____
_____
_____
_____

I AM COMMITTING TO

I will adopt a small habit of helping others by:

_____
_____
_____
_____

Date:

CHAPTER 17

HE DECIDED TO PROPOSE AT MY COMEDY SHOW

…if you can allow yourself to get to a place to change your perspective, you could see that experience was preparation, or practice if you will, for something great.

And we know that God causes everything to work together for the good of those who love God and are called according to his purpose for them.
–Romans 8:28 NLT

IMPROV

Do you believe that ALL things can work together for good? Why or why not?

PREMISE

What experience in your life seemed negative at first but really prepped you for what was coming in the future?

PUNCHLINE

Is it possible that a challenge you now have is actually preparing you for what is to come?

_____
_____
_____
_____
_____
_____

I AM COMMITTING TO

I will change my perspective of this current challenge:

_____
_____
_____

Date:

CHAPTER 18

THE TOUGHEST ROOM I EVER PLAYED

And that's when it hit me: I didn't have to depend on what a person could do for me—I just had to do my part and trust God would do His.

Do your best and let God do the rest.
–Ben Carson

IMPROV

Write about a time when you felt less than equipped to handle a situation.

PREMISE

How did the situation work out.

PUNCHLINE

How would your life be different if you depended on God instead of people?

_____
_____
_____
_____
_____
_____

I AM COMMITTING TO

I will trust God in this situation:

_____
_____
_____
_____

Date:

YOUR REFLECTIONS

Look back over your entries from this week.

What thoughts or feelings are strongest for you?

YOUR REFLECTIONS

What changes are you most proud of making?

CHAPTER 19

JUST CALL ME THE LOVE DOCTOR

Sometimes that's how we have to roll. We just need to take the next step even when we don't have everything figured out. We just have to be willing to believe it's going to work out.

Faith is taking the first step even when you don't see the whole staircase.
–Martin Luther King, Jr.

IMPROV

Write about a time when you knew you were going the right direction but could not see the whole picture.

PREMISE

Did you move forward even though you could not see, or did you let not knowing keep you from moving?

PUNCHLINE

What benefit is there to moving forward even when you can't see the whole picture? What do you lose if you don't move forward?

___

I AM COMMITTING TO

Name one step you will take even though you can't see the finish line.

___

Date:

CHAPTER 20

"I GET IT NOW"

If you want to find your purpose in life, it's important to use your talents, skills, situations, and circumstances to pursue your purpose... a.k.a., your punch line.

> *God has given each of you a gift from his great variety of spiritual gifts. Use them well to serve one another.*
> *–1 Peter 4:10 NLT*

IMPROV

Do you believe that you have gifts that can help someone else out? Why or why not?

PREMISE

Name 10 things you have done well in your life. Start in Kindergarten. Bonus points if you name more than 10.

PUNCHLINE

How can the 10 things you named be beneficial to those around you now?

_____
_____
_____
_____
_____
_____
_____

I AM COMMITTING TO

Name one person and how you can benefit them in the next 24 hours.

_____
_____
_____

Date:

CHAPTER 21

SHE STOPPED CRYING

But the solution may be easier than you think. Maybe you just need to be still and listen for your Heavenly Father's voice.

All praise to God, the Father of our Lord Jesus Christ. God is our merciful Father and the source of all comfort.
–2 Corinthians 1:3 NLT

IMPROV

Describe a time in your life when the situation seemed impossible, but the answer turned out to be simple.

PREMISE

When we consult with an authority or someone who may just have more experience in what we are going through, they make it seem easy. When have you made a situation easier for someone who did not have the experience or knowledge you have?

PUNCHLINE

Our Heavenly Father knows all and sees all. He WANTS to provide you with solutions. Have you experienced this in your life? If yes, how has it helped you? If not, what keeps you from going to Him for help?

_____
_____
_____
_____
_____
_____

I AM COMMITTING TO

Name one action you will take to look for the simple solution for your next situation:

_____
_____
_____

Date:

CHAPTER 22

THE DEAF LADY THAT MADE US LISTEN

By the way, whatever you do in life, whether at home, work, school, or wherever there are gaps—my question to you is, "Are you listening between the gaps? Are you asking what you can give, or what you can get?"

> *The most important thing in communication is to hear what isn't being said.*
> –Peter Drucker

IMPROV

What does "Hearing what is not being said" or "Listening between the gaps" mean to you?

PREMISE

How do you know when someone else is listening to what you're not saying?

PUNCHLINE

How do you think your communication success would improve if you began listening between the gaps?

_____
_____
_____
_____
_____
_____

I AM COMMITTING TO

I will approach my next conversation differently by:

_____
_____
_____
_____

Date:

CHAPTER 23

GEORGE CARLIN, MICHAEL RICHARDS, AND FORGIVENESS

A disagreement followed by forgiveness is a confirmation of love.

There is no love without forgiveness, and there is no forgiveness without love.
–Bryant H. McGill

IMPROV

What experience do you have with forgiving someone that did something truly wrong, or being forgiven for something you have done?

PREMISE

Is there someone (including yourself) that you need to forgive? What do you need to forgive them for and what is holding you back?

PUNCHLINE

How will you look at forgiveness differently in the future?

_____
_____
_____
_____
_____
_____
_____

I AM COMMITTING TO

In the future I will get forgiveness quickly by:

_____
_____
_____
_____

Date:

CHAPTER 24

FROM MY COMEDY SHOW TO PRISON

The interaction you have with someone can change the next choice they make. That next choice could change their life. Their life could change a community, and that community could change the world.

Words kill, words give life: they're either poison or fruit—you choose.
–Proverbs 18:21 MSG

IMPROV

Can you think of a time when someone impacted you in a positive way and they have no idea? Write down the lasting effect that has had on you.

PREMISE

Do you know that YOUR words have power to impact others? How does it feel to know YOU might unknowingly say something that could change someone's life?

PUNCHLINE

Will your words have a positive or negative effect on the people you come into contact with in the future?

_____
_____
_____
_____
_____
_____
_____

I AM COMMITTING TO

What is one word or phrase you use, that if removed from your vocabulary, would serve you and others better (ex: "Impossible" or "I can't do that")?

_____
_____

Date:

CHAPTER 25

THE GOOD ROOM

Just surrender to The Authority by simply opening the door and inviting God in.

> *We are not here by chance or by accident; God put us on this journey called life. We came from Him, and our greatest joy will come from giving ourselves back to Him and learning to walk with Him every day until we return to Him.*
> *–Billy Graham*

IMPROV

Some of us have that one "Good Room" in our house that we show guests. But God knows about all the other rooms and loves us anyway. Have you let God into ALL of your life?

PREMISE

If you had to measure (using a percentage) how much of your life God is allowed into, what would that look like? What keeps you from raising this bar?

PUNCHLINE

How much better would your life be if you were to let Him into the WHOLE thing?

_____
_____
_____
_____
_____
_____
_____

I AM COMMITTING TO

I will open the door wider for God by:

_____
_____
_____
_____

Date:

YOUR REFLECTIONS

Look back over your entries from this week.

What thoughts or feelings are strongest for you?

_____
_____
_____
_____
_____
_____
_____
_____
_____
_____
_____
_____
_____
_____
_____
_____

YOUR REFLECTIONS

What changes are you most proud of making?

Ready for More?

Funny How My Life Works course is a course where you get to watch me tell you some stories from my book, and add some details that are not shared in the book. I tell my stories. You add your stories. You discover yourself in a deeper way than you thought possible.

This course will cause you to think and take action. It will put you in position to help other people, too.

It's a course like no other course. Because there's funny, of course, and the stories take us on a ride, allowing us to receive much more than just informatio —Boom!
Funny How My Life Works will help you get your life on course.

And it's funny. Of course.

Check out our course at FunnyHowMyLifeWorks.com

Get your weekly dose of inspiration wrapped in funny.
Subscribe now to the *Funny How Life Works* Podcast where we use funny to teach people how life works!